JOURNEY
TO THE TROPICS

The Adventures of a Short Term Mission Trip to the
Philippines

As told through the eyes of R. A. Beaulacotte
and co-authored by Beaulacotte Sr.

Glorious Vision Publications
Massillon, OH

JOURNEY
TO THE TROPICS

Table of Contents

A NOTE FROM THE AUTHORS

Dear reader, through the following pages, I hope that you will see how exciting it is to serve the Lord Jesus Christ. My prayer is that as you read my story, you too will be stirred up to see what God has planned for your life. I personally needed to go on this mission trip to the Philippines for God to teach me how to wait on His timing. This trip also stoked the flame of my burden for missions. Most of all, it brought me to a point where I chose to follow Christ even if it meant losing my life.

I benefitted by going on this mission trip by seeing a missionary in live action making the most of his time. He had a compassion for souls and a passion to see them saved. It convicted me to make better use of my time on a regular basis. I matured by learning patience and humbling myself to be a servant in any situation. Over and over I find that God is not looking for men of great stature, He is looking for weak vessels who are willing to yield to His power. May you too find the joy of serving Jesus with complete surrender to His sweet will.

-R. A. Beaulacotte

Looking back, I am glad that I went on this mission trip to the Philippines. It was such a blessing to have gone with my son. Although it was exciting to plan for the trip, I have to admit that I had a moment of fear. The Lord is quite willing at times to allow a believer to be "pressed out of measure, above strength" (2 Corinthians 1:8), but not beyond the strength of God. Just days before we were to go, I sat alone on a bench in my garage and told God, "I cannot do this." As I continued to sit alone, I was reminded of verses I had read earlier in the day from the Pauline Epistles. Paul put no confidence in his flesh. I finally said to God, "Okay, I will go; but I will need you to help me do this." If you let God, you too will find that His "strength is made perfect in weakness" (2 Corinthians 12:9). There are things that God has for each of us which are well beyond anything we can ever envision. I challenge you to simply make yourself available to God, trust Him, and see what the Lord can do with a vessel surrendered to His plans.

- Beaulacotte Sr.

CHAPTER ONE

What Can God Do with a Mission Trip?

"Mine eye affecteth mine heart…"
Lamentations 3:51

The reader may be wondering, "What is so great about a mission trip?" After all, most of the stories we hear are about sleeping in uncomfortable places, eating strange food, smelling odd scents, and seeing unusual things. What value is there in being inconvenienced?

There is great value in a mission trip because of its ability to push individuals closer to God. Enduring peculiar environments does not in and of itself produce spirituality, but it should leave us leaning on the Lord. When one is stretched beyond his ability, that should push him to draw strength from Christ. When someone's pride is cut down because he does not know what to do, that is an opportunity for God to teach him humility. The value is not so much found in the circumstances themselves as much as in the result of the circumstances.

There are different places of the world, where God can teach people certain lessons more effectively. For example, in poverty-stricken places, we should leave being more thankful for America's blessings. Some things can only be learned overseas.

Taking note of other believers' sacrifices and joy should convict us to be more surrendered to the Lord. In communist controlled areas, we should leave being more thankful for the liberty we enjoy in the United States. Christians' struggles and steadfast commitment ought to make us more devoted to our Saviour. Observing other believers' dedication to Christ might even stir someone up to be a missionary to places where there is no gospel witness. What you see on a mission trip will affect your heart and life forever.

Seeing that God can provide necessary funds, and seeing that God can open doors in miraculous manners, why is there a lack of individuals taking mission trips? I believe there are two main reasons. First, it is too inconvenient to interrupt one's school, job, family plans, etc. Second, people are scared of the unknown. Some fears are legitimate, but other fears are no better than crippling diseases. I believe that many people do not take a mission trip simply because they are unwilling.

Please read on through my story. I do not hide the facts. Some fears are legitimate. Inconveniences are real. Disease is possible. Problems happen. I will not pretend and hide the truth from you. But by the end of reading my story, I hope that you will realize the value of taking a mission trip and make the decision to serve the Lord no matter what. In spite of hardships and hazards, it is an amazingly blessed adventure to serve Jesus with your life- even if there is a chance of dying.

- R. A. Beaulacotte

The Lord used the two mission trips with my son (going to Nepal and to the Philippines) to really change my life's direction in many facets. They allowed me to experience God's divine viewpoint of the world. God is a big God and He is worshipped in many different outward forms by people of diverse cultures. The trips also helped give me a needed eternal perspective of my service for Jesus. It awakened my need to consciously yield to the Lord.

The experiences in the Philippines especially helped me with Bible study, Bible teaching, outreach, prioritizing my life, and checking my motives for how I live. Without a doubt, having these experiences with my son really helped me accept and support God's choosing him for service as a missionary. Although a mission trip may plant the seed in someone to later become a missionary, that certainly is not the case for all who go. However, at the very least, a mission trip is capable of drawing you closer to God and changing your life forever.

- Beaulacotte Sr.

CHAPTER TWO

Setting the Stage

"But as it is written, Eye hath not seen, nor ear heard, neither have entered into the heart of man, the things which God hath prepared for them that love him."
1 Corinthians 2:9

The events that follow are our personal testimonies. Everything is true and accurate to the best of our memories. Person's names have been substituted to protect the individuals.

I grew up in a Christian home, got saved when I was about seven years old, and later God called me to preach in my early teenage years. When I was fifteen and a half, my family moved from California to Hawaii in February of 2014. After turning sixteen years old, I began my junior year of Highschool. Being homeschooled, I had excelled in some subjects and chose to take on a couple more in order to complete my junior and senior year together.

During that fall semester, I took a mission trip to Nepal that greatly inspired me to serve God with my life. As spring 2015 came around, and thus graduation from Highschool, I was faced with a number of life decisions. I needed to choose working toward a career path or going to college. I had to choose whether I would go to college nearby or go away to college.

Over the early summer months, the Lord directed me to go to Bible college in Ohio. As my first fall semester in college came to a close, God led me to be a missionary. That leading by God occurred only fourteen months after my trip to Nepal. I can look back and see how God used my Nepal trip to show me the need for foreign mission work. It was a seed that came to fruition in my college days.

In college, I began to get to know a young lady with whom I was attending church and our relationship grew to a close friendship. She would later become my wife after I graduated college. But before leaving college to come home for summer break, she gave me a book as a parting gift. It happened to be about how God uses suffering to grow us. The book also showed how we can take our physical tribulations and turn it around for God's glory. I had no idea how important it would be for me to read that book while flying home. I went home to my family in Hawaii with great plans of my own- but they were not God's plans.

My perfect little summer plan involved me getting a construction job and earning a bunch of money to help pay for college and a future family. But early on, I ran into a number of accidents. For starters, in my family's back yard, my dad was growing bananas. He needed my help catching them as he cut the stock of the bunch. I was standing below looking up when I got a drip of sticky banana sap in my eye that required a trip to stat care. With plenty of flushing, my eye was good in a couple of days, but it initially delayed my plan to get in touch with the construction contractor.

Then within a couple of weeks, I was out on the beach playing with my skim board. I was ambition to get back in shape and to be able to do flips off of it when I hit the surf. (As a disclaimer, I do believe in maintaining modesty while enjoying God's creation). On this particular day, I began to get tired and misjudged a wave. When I attempted the front flip, I fell sideways into shallow water and landed on my left shoulder. It too merited a trip to stat care as well as X-rays. The fall separated my acromioclavicular (AC) joint in my left should and I had to go through a few weeks of physical therapy at home. This completely ended any opportunity to work a construction job over the summer. In fact, to this day I still get sore in my AC joint area when I overuse my left arm. What a great summer plan I had... but it was not God's summer plan for me.

As it got close to the end of June 2016, I was sitting by myself thinking about how nothing was turning out right. Everything I planned was going wrong. I felt unproductive. My dad came outside to talk with me. I was sitting in despair and voiced my complaint to my dad, "I feel like I'm not doing anything worthwhile. I feel like my summer is just going to waste." He replied with a very out of the blue response, "How would you like to take a mission trip?" My face lit up and he could see it as I replied, "Yeah! That would be great!" God was closing the doors on all of my plans to bring me to the point of walking through the only open door left- His door.

This interaction between my dad and me took place on a Saturday evening. My dad suggested that we go to church the next day and see if there was a supported missionary that our pastor thought would be a good one for us to go visit. Pastor recommended Bro. Rod, a missionary in the Philippines, who was related to some folks in our church.

We talked with the family of Bro. Rod and asked if it would work for us to go visit him. Their response was that they would contact him and check. Early in the week we were contacted and told that if we booked the plane flights, Bro. Rod would take care of the rest. On Wednesday of that week, we booked our flights. In the Wednesday evening church service, we shared our itinerary with the family at church so that they could pass it on to him. We would have to leave the very next week.

I must here interject into the story a crucial part of our deciding when to go and how God mercifully directed. My brother and sister-in-law were to be graduating from a police academy and we did not want to miss their graduation. We pretty much had two weeks prior to their graduation or two weeks following their graduation. The two weeks following would have put the time frame really close to my having to go back to school, so we chose the earlier two weeks. That put our departure taking place in seven days.

It was twelve days from the time that we initially tossed out the idea of a mission trip to the day we boarded our flights! The Lord in advance had blessed us with the means and we both had passports from our trip to Nepal. Because the Philippines would give us a visa upon arrival, we did not have to do any advance paperwork. Since Bro. Rod was going to take care of everything, that cut out the part of transportation and hotel arrangements.

The only way to describe this trip is that God was at work. 2 Chronicles 29:36 says, "And Hezekiah rejoiced, and all the people, that God had prepared the people: for the thing was done suddenly." This is how we felt. God had prepared us and now He was at work bringing the whole trip about quickly. I do not recommend taking a mission trip this fast and unexpected. But if God is at work, we need to be ready to trust and obey at a moment's notice. With the Lord, trips can come about quickly, but it must be because God is in it, not because we are trying to rush something.

Getting ready for takeoff

CHAPTER THREE

Beginning Travel and Initial Arrival

"My grace is sufficient for thee: for my strength is
made perfect in weakness."
2 Corinthians 12:9

"We left Maui early in the morning headed to
the Philippines. We had no idea where we would stay,
what we would do, where we would go, who we
would be with, or what we would eat. Just faith that
we would meet Brother Rod at the airport whom we
had never met nor talked to before," (Beaulacotte
Sr.).

Our full trip lasted from July 6 to July 20,
2016. From Honolulu to our layover in Guam, we
flew over the Mariana Trench which is the deepest
part of the earth. Our plane ride during the first half
was smooth but then it got bumpy because of a
typhoon in the area. My stomach sure appreciated
being back on solid ground for a time.

When we arrived in the Philippines late
Thursday night, one of our checked luggage bags was
missing. We were told that it must not have left
Guam. We had to fill out some paperwork and then
finally met up with the missionary, Brother Rod.

For anyone traveling overseas, it is always recommended to have everything you initially need in your carry-on, including a change of clothes, because occasionally bags do get delayed or sometimes lost permanently. Bro. Rod and one of his sons picked us up and began driving toward our destination. Theoretically, the drive should only have been three and a half hours. About two hours down the road in congested traffic, we got a call from the airport that our bag was found. We turned around, picked it up, and then headed for the hotel again. We got in at about five in the morning on Friday, July 8th.

Since the Philippines is eighteen hours ahead of Hawaii's time zone, our actual length of travel was only about twenty-nine hours of flying and driving. To lie horizontal felt so good, even if it was only for an hour and a half. But before I went to sleep, I had a most unusual experience. I was brushing my teeth and my mouth started going numb. I could not figure out what was going on until I examined my tooth paste a little closer. I was brushing my teeth with hydrocortisone anti-itch cream! No wonder it tasted slightly odd.

Prepare to function on the strength of God if you travel overseas because of sleep deprivation and ministry fatigue. Friday, July 8th, we only had about an hour and a half of sleep before needing to get up for breakfast. We had a schedule to keep because folks were hungry for the Word of God.

Our first appointment was at eight in the morning at a motorcycle shop. The owner and his workers start each day with Bible study before they open up. My dad gave the message and at the end Bro. Rod summarized it in Tagalog, the national language of the Philippines. Bro. Rod expressed his desire to one day buy a tricycle that can haul six people for "bus ministry." Thankfully, we were able to get a little rest before going on a social visit in the evening.

After a mid-day nap, we went to the municipality of Calasiao. My sister-in-law is from the Philippines and we got to meet her family. Filipinos use the word, "balai" to refer to the parents of one's son-in-law/daughter-in-law. Thus, my dad met his balai and vice versa.

In our social interactions, we learned the difference between pet dogs and wild dogs. Pet dogs get their tails cropped to show they have someone taking care of them. Wild dogs have full tails and are free game for the eating.

We also got to try some foods that are unique to the Philippines. We had Polvoron which are a kind of short bread cookie. We got to drink Cobra which is a citrus energy drink (and much needed at this point of our trip). Rice and noodles made up the majority of the meal, but I also got to eat balut. One of my sister-in-law's brothers saw me put the egg on my plate, he asked if I knew what it was. I think it surprised him when I told him yes and that I had eaten it once before.

For those who do not know, balut is a fertilized duck egg, partially developed, and then boiled to be eaten. Most folks cannot get past the thought of it. For those who can, one then has to get past the smell of it. But once you dive in, it is like having the most tender pulled beef you can imagine with a side of hard egg yolk in a warm broth. Add some salt and it's pretty good… as long as you do not get any feathers or bones. As an American, I do not personally crave balut, but it tastes perfectly fine and is not something to be afraid of if you happen to go overseas to the Philippines.

The most exciting part about my extended in-laws is that they have converted from Catholics to Christians. My sister-in-law's parents had been out of the Catholic church for about two years because they started reading the Bible for themselves. They came to realize that their works could not save them, and they trusted in Jesus for their salvation. Galatians 2:16 says, "Knowing that a man is not justified by the works of the law, but by the faith of Jesus Christ, even we have believed in Jesus Christ, that we might be justified by the faith of Christ, and not by the works of the law: for by the works of the law shall no flesh be justified."

My extended in-laws also had begun studying God's Word together with their friends. On this occasion they had lots of their family and friends come over so we could have Bible study with them. It reminded me of Cornelius, in Acts 10, calling together his family and friends to hear the gospel preached by the apostle Peter.

After my dad gave a Bible lesson, Bro. Rod carried on most of the conversation in Tagalog to discuss some doctrinal differences between Catholicism and Biblical Christianity. Most importantly they discussed how to have assurance of salvation. Catholics have no such assurance because their religion is works based. But those who put their faith in Christ can have one hundred percent assurance of their salvation because the work of salvation was already accomplished when Jesus died for our sins and rose again.

Filipino meal with balut duck egg

CHAPTER FOUR

My Personal Struggle

"Faithful is he that calleth you, who also will do it."
1 Thessalonians 5:24

On Saturday, July 9th, 2016, we began our day by going to a restaurant where businessman gather for breakfast and a challenge from God's Word. My dad brought the message on how to be a good manager. A good manager responsibly handles personal mistakes. It was a very profitable time and my dad's long career history enabled him to connect with the folks in a special way.

From there we had intended to go have an outdoor children's ministry where I was to teach, but the rain initially hindered us, and we had to be flexible and allow a change of plans. Instead we were able to view a plot of land where a building could potentially be erected for a new church plant. After viewing the land, we went to a kidney dialysis center and my dad had the opportunity to preach the gospel to the patients. Some will recover and some might not. We felt the heavy burden of sharing the good news before it is too late as folks die and descend to the depths of hell. After lunch, we had a quick break to go back to our hotel.

Here in the middle of our second day in the Philippines, I came face to face with an ugly side of myself. My dad had gotten to speak four times already, and I had spoken none. Later this day I was to teach the children while my dad would teach adults. My dad was also preparing to teach a Bible study this night in someone's home. My feelings were wrong, but they were so real.

I felt jealous. I had pride. I was dealing with anger. I longed to preach, but I saw the opportunities to speak given to someone else. I felt as though my youthfulness was being despised. Here my dad got all the important speaking opportunities and all I was given was children's ministry. It seemed like I was viewed as a mere boy that could not preach to adults. I had prideful thoughts like, "Am not I the one who is called to preach? Am not I the one led to be a missionary?" I found a tendency to complain against God. I know those feelings were wrong, but they were so real. I was doing the best to hide them from everyone around me.

This is where the rubber meets the roads. This is the kind of struggle where God teaches you things in the private times on a mission trip. I had an enemy, Satan, walking about as a roaring lion seeking to devour me, and I had the internal enemy of my own flesh. This intense struggle could have destroyed the spirit of our entire trip. Everything to come could have been viewed through a bitter spirit and a sour attitude. As always, prayer and the Word of God was the solution.

As I turned in my Bible, I was reminded that I have no right to complain. Jesus saved me from my sins, from judgment, and from the Lake of Fire. I ought to be grateful as there is no room to complain in light of how good Christ has been to me. Preaching and ministering is not and cannot be about me. The Scripture says in John 3:30, "He must increase, but I must decrease." Ministry is not about what I get to do, but about Jesus getting the glory. Matthew 6:10 reminded me that our prayer ought to be, "Thy kingdom come. Thy will be done in earth, as it is in heaven." The will of God is not only something that needs to be done in the earth, but also within me. Finally, the greatest answer from God came from 1 Thessalonians 5:24, "Faithful is he that calleth you, who also will do it."

I acknowledged that yes, God called me to preach. Yes, God called me to be a missionary. But it is also the Lord who chooses when I preach, how I preach, to whom I preach, and where I preach. Although this spiritual struggle was extremely intense, by the comfort of the Scriptures I was able to move on with a calm surrender. God is God. He can do as He pleases.

This lesson was of extreme importance for me to learn. When I came face to face with possible death, I had a composed assurance that the Lord can do with me whatever He pleases. But I also know that every time I am asked by a pastor to preach, that God will work with me. Since the Lord called me to preach, then the opportunities to preach are sovereignly chosen by God. And when I preach, God will be with me to perform that which He has called me to do.

My dark valley of spiritual warfare has since become one of the greatest mountains of victory. Whereas the devil sought to destroy me, God used this experience to make me stronger. I do not know how God could have so effectively taught me this life lesson except in this mission trip situation.

After lunch, the rain held off enough that we were able to go to the dumpsite and cemetery. These people are in such poverty that they actually live in the dump. My dad had the opportunity to preach the gospel to a group of adults, and I was privileged to teach a lesson to the children. We were gathered in a three-sided covering with some children sitting on top of the above-ground stone tomb. Multiple folks expressed the desire to be saved but it is hard to know how many and who as the deeper spiritual matters were discussed in their heart language- Tagalog.

In the evening, we went to a house for a home Bible study and supper. My dad taught on what a true disciple of Jesus looks like. My dad's balai were also there which was an added blessing.

Ministry at the cemetery

CHAPTER FIVE

Tag Team Ministry Opportunities

"For we are labourers together with God…"
1 Corinthians 3:9a

On Sunday, July 10th, our day started rather early with breakfast at 6:30 a.m. The first church that we went to was still in a planting stage. Bro. Rod was technically pastoring it while they looked for someone else to take over the work. My dad preached for this church during their 7:30 a.m. service. It was exciting to listen to them express the need to add on because of their children's ministry growing so large.

At 9 a.m., I was privileged to teach the adult Sunday school hour at Bro. Rod's main church that he pastors. While he may carry something of a pastoral title, he certainly lives and serves more like a missionary. My dad preached the 10 a.m. service on the subject of revival. We were able to go out for lunch and fellowship with Bro. Rod and his family before engaging in further afternoon ministries.

At 3 p.m., I got to preach to a group of youth exhorting them to live for Christ. Then at 4 p.m., my dad got to preach to families on the subject of a Christian home. During this time, we began to have monsoon rains for about two days straight. Apparently, if the water gets high enough, they can have fish swim down the streets.

Monday, July 11th, was spent mostly traveling to the neighboring island, Panay. We were going to stay with a family and minister alongside another pastor. I think it is here convenient to share that I was not the only one struggling with the matter of speaking opportunities. My dad felt uncomfortable with how much he was being pushed into the speaking engagements. From my dad's perspective, he viewed the trip as being for me. He knew God's calling on my life and leading in my life. He wanted me to get more firsthand experience as well. Without sharing my struggles with him, my dad brought up to me his discomfort about the situation and we decided to take turns as best we could.

Looking back, I can see the hand of God directing with such grace and glory. When Bro. Rod brought up future preaching engagements, my dad advocated when he and I would take turns. In my youthfulness, it was not my place to ask for more preaching opportunities. Yet when I learned to rest my confidence on God's timing, the Lord placed the opportunities in my lap.

Although Tuesday, July 12th, was the only full day we had on the island of Panay, we sure experienced a lot. Our hosts were an older couple and went by the names Tata and Nana (equivalent to Grandpa and Grandma in English terminology). Calling our hosts Tata and Nana was not weird to us because the Hawaiian culture also utilizes family relationship terminology outside of familial boundaries.

Tata took us for a walk up the street to where the church had cleared some land to begin building. At the time of our trip, Pastor Re and the church were meeting in Tata's garage but has since been able to move into their building. The rest of the morning was spent with Pastor Re doing street preaching, but it was not like American street preaching.

Bro. Rod, his son, Pastor Re, my dad, and I all piled into a Filipino tricycle called a "tuktuk". Two in the cab and three in the bed. Pastor Re had rigged a microphone up to a loudspeaker mounted on top of his tuktuk. With one hand we held the mic, and with the other hand we held our Bibles. However, needing two hands to turn to passages left us preaching completely from memorized Scriptures. The simple gospel message was our glorious theme. I am reminded of what the Apostle Paul said in Romans 1:15, "So, as much as in me is, I am ready to preach the gospel…"

I preached first at a small bus stop, then my dad preached at a little market, and last of all I preached to an invisible audience. We had stopped along the side of a road with jungle-like growth on both sides. Pastor Re told us that the growth of vegetation was the backyards of houses out of sight. Here I preached into the open air with the hope that folks would be listening in on the message of salvation.

In the afternoon, we went to a market area and checked out souvenirs. Then in the evening, we had church at Tata's house. I preached and my dad gave his testimony about being saved out of Catholicism.

After the church service, we learned the hard way that unless rice is present, it is not a meal. The church fellowshipped over a snack of flavorful noodles and buttered bread. I had one plate and was urged to have another. After my second plate, I ended up taking a little more. The food was delicious, and I was full. About the time that I finished eating, our host came out and told us that supper was ready. Supper? What was all this food I just ate? Inside on the table was a full spread of all sorts of food. My dad and I looked at each other with trembling. We did our best to show our appreciation by trying a little of each food as we stuffed our already full stomachs. Looking back on that evening, we can only laugh.

Wednesday, July 13th, was a completely full day of traveling. We flew back to the Manila airport on the island of Luzon. We then spent ten hours driving north to Isabela. The first couple hours were spent crawling out of rush hour traffic. The remaining hours were spent mostly on winding roads behind slow big rigs. At last we got some rest and prepared for the second half of our trip.

Open air market

CHAPTER SIX

The Second Half

"This sickness is not unto death, but for the glory of God, that the Son of God might be glorified thereby."
John 11:4

So as not to belabor the account of our trip and to proceed to further areas in which the hand of God was clearly seen to be at work in us and around us, I will attempt to keep the following details brief. July 14th began by attending a pastor's conference. One of the pastors who were present was named Bro. Andrew. Our church in Hawaii assisted him and his congregation with some funds to purchase land for a building to be built. After lunch, we visited Mrs. Nel at her farm where we got to pick dragon fruit right off the plants. It was pretty neat, but we were warned to watch out for cobras that like the sweet fruit too. Mrs. Nel invited some of her friends over and we had a Bible study before supper. Most of them were staunch Catholics and again my dad was able to share his testimony about being saved out of Catholicism. We held another Bible study late in the evening at Mrs. Fra's house as well.

On Friday, July 15th, we traveled about six hours back to the area out of which we were basing. In the evening we had supper with a church family where we also had a time of Bible study and prayer. July 16th was a little busier. We had breakfast and Bible study with the group of businessmen again. Then at Bro. Rod's main church, we held a children's evangelistic program. Lunch was spent with another church family where we had a time of prayer with them. The afternoon and evening were spent at the house of my dad's balai. We held a Bible study followed by a birthday party for one of the grandchildren.

On Sunday, July 17th, I began to feel ill. In spite of this, the day's demands were not diminished. If anything, Sunday is the busiest day in the life of God's servants. I preached the early morning message at the first church. My dad preached the Sunday school message at Bro. Rod's main church. Then I preached the main morning service. For lunch, we went out to eat with Bro. Rod's family and another church family. We returned to the church building for a large evangelistic outreach service. It was originally scheduled for 3 p.m., but people were on island time. We went door to door nearby passing out tracts while waiting for more folks to show up. At 5 p.m., we started the service and there was a good turnout of people. By the end of the day, I began to have a continual fever except for when I was on acetaminophen.

I spent Monday, July 18th, with a somewhat weak stomach. At 8 a.m., we went to the police station to hold Bible study before the officers began their shift. Since my brother and sister-in-law were going through the police academy back home, my dad was able to connect with the officers in a special way. At 9 a.m., we went to the BIR office (equivalent to the Internal Revenue Service within the United States) and held a time of prayer with the department director! How neat it was to observe true religion penetrating into secular governmental business. The remainder of our day was spent visiting with multiple families, saying farewell, and eating way too many times. By the end of the day, my dad's stomach turned weak also. We began to figure my fever and fatigue was related to something we had both eaten, but that was far from the truth.

On Tuesday, July 19th, our morning ministry plans were cut out due to not feeling the best. We spent the time saying goodbye to my dad's balai and packing some things from Bro. Rod for us to take back to his relatives in our home church. At 1 p.m., we began the six-hour drive to the airport, mostly in rush hour traffic. Our flight was scheduled to depart at 11:30 p.m. that night, but delays caused us not to leave until 2 a.m. on Wednesday. Our delays leaving Manila caused us to miss our connecting flight and we were laid over in Guam for a whole day. Finally, we made it home to Hawaii on Wednesday at around 9:30 p.m. Again, the time traveling was many hours. Combining my fever, stomach problems, and sleep deprivation left me feeling half alive.

Children's ministry at church

Person to person evangelism

CHAPTER SEVEN

In the Shadow of Death

"For the work of Christ he was nigh unto death…"
Philippians 2:30

On Thursday, July 21st, we were able to attend my brother and sister-in-law's police academy graduation. While on ibuprofen, I felt as good as if I were not sick; but without it, I felt horrible. On the next day, a gland under my jawbone began to swell and it put us on the search for what this mystery disease was. By Saturday morning, the swelling extended part way down my neck. On Saturday, July 23rd, we went to the stat care office as a beginning start, but the doctors were not sure what it was and sent me home to rest up. I did not go to church on Sunday because I had a high fever.

Things were obviously not getting better and we went back to stat care on Monday to get a test for white blood cell count and a mumps blood test. We went back again on Tuesday to expand the testing to a throat culture and a blood test for mononucleosis. I have no idea how the tests panned out because I was in surgery long before the results came back. I suspect they were negative as the surgery revealed the true disease.

On Tuesday evening, July 26th, my throat began to swell to the point of feeling like partially choking on my own throat when I swallowed. My airway was collapsing from the swelling and I had a hard time not panicking. My mom was out of the house, but as soon as she got home, we went to the emergency room around 8:30 p.m. At the hospital, I got a CT scan and blood work again. A doctor came into my room and explained that I had a swollen lymph node that needed removed. After signing the waver releasing the hospital from liability should I die while under their care, I was wheeled to the anesthesiologist and then into the operating room. My parents were the only ones present for me to tell them that I loved them. I had no idea if I would survive. Sure, doctors put people under and perform surgeries for a living, but there is a reason why I had to sign that waver. Sometimes folks do not survive. On the one hand, I was really scared. I wondered if my life was really at the end. On the other hand, I knew that my times were in the hand of God. I knew Jesus as my Saviour, and I knew that death was only the portal into glory.

On Wednesday, July 27th, for a brief period, I was awakened from the anesthesia to gag out the breathing tube shoved down my throat prior to surgery. The next thing I remember was seeing my parents in the intensive care unit (ICU) with me. I was unable to talk at all. I had to use pen and paper to communicate. After I got better, I found out that my beautiful penmanship was mostly only scribbles. On Wednesday night, I was transferred to a regular hospital room for the remainder of my stay.

On Thursday, I was able to go for walks at the hospital with my mom and dad, but I was very tired. By Friday, I felt like breaking out of the hospital had I not gotten released.   These few days in the hospital were rather miserable. I was lonely and really bored. The hospital in which I stayed was also not conducive to getting any good rest. During this time, I fell in love with Psalm 118, and Psalm 119. The Scriptures quickened me. God's Word was my comfort. I am grateful that I had access to a Bible which was such a help to me physically, mentally, emotionally, and especially spiritually.

Because the surgery removed the mass from my neck, I was left with a void hole. For recovery purposes I had a drainage tube going into the side of my neck to prevent the hole from filling with fluid. On Friday morning, July 29th, the doctor removed the tube from my neck. That evening, I was released to go home and get some real rest. Through the autopsy afterward, we learned that my sickness had been streptococcus type A. It had killed one of my lymph nodes, got inside, and was able to grow without attack from my natural immune system. My road to recovery was about four months long. It lasted both at home and even in college. Even prior to going back to college, I had to get my wound cut open one more time to drain a buildup of fluid.

God has been good to me over the months and years. I have fully recovered from this incident other than a scar that serves to remind me that I am living on borrowed time. While some may consider this a negative thing in my life, I view it as a blessing. I am more conscious to use my time wisely. The scar has also become a conversation point that has led into me being able to share about the goodness of the Lord. If you let God work, He can turn your weaknesses into steppingstones of strength.

CHAPTER EIGHT

God's Love Is the Believer's Hope

"Choose you this day whom ye will serve…"
Joshua 24:15

About now, the reader may feel justified in not taking a mission trip. The reader may say, "See, that is why I refuse to serve God with my life." But may I remind you that accidents happen all the time. Folks die from all sorts of diseases and mishaps. Turn your attention to the goodness of God.

Look at how the Lord orchestrated the trip so that I could be home (instead of in a foreign country) to have the surgery and recover enough from surgery that I could still go to college within a couple weeks. Observe the mercy of Christ to spare my life when I could have died. Take note of the life lessons Jesus taught me along the journey. Looking back on this trip, I can honestly say with Paul in Romans 11:33, "O the depth of the riches both of the wisdom and knowledge of God! how unsearchable are his judgments, and his ways past finding out!" I entered my summer completely unaware that God wanted me to go on a mission trip. Even though I was ignorant to God's ways, He still directed my path in His divine wisdom and according to His great mercy.

Looking ahead, the reader may think that I should stop serving God lest I come close to death again. But I want you to consider that we live in a world of accidents, disease, problems, trials, hardships, heartaches, and death. We cannot avoid the world in which we live. We will face these issues whether or not we serve Jesus with our lives. I hope the reader will see that serving God brings with it a lot of extra benefits while we live. And even if we should die in the service of the King, what better way to live our lives? For a believer in Christ, our anchor of hope rests in the love of God.

Who shall separate us from the love of Christ? shall tribulation, or distress, or persecution, or famine, or nakedness, or peril, or sword? As it is written, For thy sake we are killed all the day long; we are accounted as sheep for the slaughter. Nay, in all these things we are more than conquerors through him that loved us. For I am persuaded, that neither death, nor life, nor angels, nor principalities, nor powers, nor things present, nor things to come, Nor height, nor depth, nor any other creature, shall be able to separate us from the love of God, which is in Christ Jesus our Lord.

Romans 8:35-39

I serve God with the calm assurance that nothing can separate me from His love. This can be your confidence in service too. What a precious Saviour is Jesus! The highest praise is due His name. Jesus is worthy of the mightiest service. Christ deserves our entire love.

This of course, is easier said than done. Though I have chosen to serve God with my life, it is a choice that must be made every day. Less than three months after returning from the Philippines, the Lord led me to be a missionary to Central Asia. I wrestled with God for two days telling Him "No." I was scared of the unknown that it could entail. It is easy to say that I am living on borrowed time. It is easy to say that God deserves my whole life. It is easy to say that I ought to be a living sacrifice for the Lord. But I still had to make the decision to trust God. I still had to choose to serve God even if it could mean losing my life or facing persecution. After I surrendered to follow Christ's leading me to Asia, He gave me a peace that passes all understanding. God gave me the calm assurance that His love would never forsake me and that His grace would always be sufficient to meet every need.

Each of us have one, and only one life to live. Because we only have one life, it is the most precious life that we have. I cannot think of a better way to use my life than living every day to know Christ and make Him known to others.

So, how will you use your life? Will you serve God? Will you choose to serve Christ no matter what? Will you decide that living for Jesus is worth your whole life, even if it could mean losing your life?

I have made those decisions and strive to continue making those decisions every day. I hope that you will choose to serve God also no matter what. I hope the reader will find out what a blessed adventure it is to serve God with complete surrender to His sweet will.

CHAPTER NINE

If You Choose to Take a Mission Trip

"Behold, I say unto you, Lift up your eyes, and look on the fields; for they are white already to harvest."
John 4:35b

Dear Young People,
Please consider taking a mission trip. Open your eyes to a world that is bigger than your hometown. You have a life ahead of you that can be used in wondrous ways for the Lord if you let Him. Following the will of God is life's greatest adventure and contains no regrets.

Dear Parents,
Please see the value of a young person taking a mission trip as one of life's greatest privileges. You never know how Christ will use it. The time, money, and effort are a price well worth the life-long benefits. If possible, go with them. It is easier to return from overseas and have at least one person who understands everything that was experienced, but that will only happen if you go also. My trip to Nepal was also one of the greatest bonding times between me and my dad, not just in the moment, but forever because we now share a common experience that no one else does.

Dear Pastors and Those Who Oversee the Youth in Church,

Please urge your youth to take an overseas mission trip to an economically third-world country. It will shake their life and draw them closer to Jesus. If your church does not do mission trips, seek out a trustworthy church that does. If I may also encourage you, go along yourself and see God at work. Mission trips are not just a benefit to young people, they benefit all people.

I can hear the responses already. That trip was great for you, but I do not have the finances. Trips are for youth and I am too old. I do not have a church that does missions. I cannot go overseas because I do not have a passport. I have too many responsibilities at home to attend to. I don't know where to begin. My friend, this chapter is for you as I guide you through overcoming common obstacles. Many obstacles can easily be overcome. But may I warn you that the hardest obstacle of all is quitting. Only you can make the decision that by God's grace you will not quit.

Where to Begin?

1.   PRAYER. I cannot stress enough the importance of prayer at every stage of planning. In the excitement of a trip, you might barrel along and miss out on the blessings God has for you by staying where you are. I know that I have highly recommended and urged the reader to take a mission trip, but it must be done on God's timetable and to the Lord's destination. Not every mission trip is a success, but every mission trip directed by God is more of a success than imaginable. Do not forget to pray.

2.   Where is there a need? The focus of a mission trip must be to serve the Lord by serving others. Pray about a missionary already on the field that you can assist. Maybe you can ask some friends. Maybe your church already supports some missionaries that you can get in contact with. Enlist the help of your spiritual mentors.

3.   Once you get a general idea about what country you are going to, then you can begin making a detailed plan.

Create a Plan

*Disclaimer: the following personal suggestions are from experiences prior to Covid-19. Please be aware that international travel is in fluctuation at the time of this publication.

1.   Use the internet to your advantage. You need to determine an estimated cost of airfare. Always round things higher because you will have to pay taxes, fees, and suggested insurance above the cost of your ticket. Depending on the airline, you will also have to pay for checked luggage.

2.   If you do not have a passport, you will need one. Passports are processed through the United States Postal Service. You can consult them for current fees and details. Some offices will take your photo, and some may require you to bring in your own (according to their specifications). Get in touch with them to receive the most current details.

3.	Plan ahead. Depending on the country, an entrance visa can be processed in the airport upon your arrival into the foreign country. For other countries, you may need to apply for your visa ahead of time. Each country has different types of entrance visas and you will need to decide what is the best for you. There are some good online websites to apply for visas. I recommend getting the concierge service for an additional fee. They helped me prepare my application. By using a known service, it can also help ensure that the application is accepted. If you have to apply for a visa ahead of time, you will have to send in your passport by mail; the visa will also have to be processed within a certain time frame in relation to your scheduled departure.

4.	If you are going to visit a missionary on the field, that is a true blessing as you figure out the cost of food and lodging. The missionary may put you up somewhere or at least give a recommendation. Missionaries are taught to be hospitable, but you should not take advantage of them. If he/she offers to take care of things, insist on paying your way. Be a blessing, not a burden during your stay. Go with the heart of a servant and you will both be blessed. Do not forget that airport food can cost about three times as much as normal.

5.	Build into your budget a cushion for emergencies, unforeseen expenses, and souvenirs. The country and number of people going are the biggest factors in determining this cushion.

6.	Travel	Insurance	is	highly recommended.

7.   Check with your local health department to see if any vaccines are required before going on your trip. Some vaccines require multiple doses to be effective. If vaccines are not required, you may still choose to get certain ones just to be cautious.

Picking a Time of Year
1.   When is it convenient for the missionary to have you visit?
2.   Prices of airfare fluctuate based on the time of year.
3.   When is the weather generally favorable for travel and outdoor ministry?
4.   These are three primary factors that affect trip dates. I also do not recommend planning a trip sooner than six months away.

Raising the Funds
At this stage, you should know where you are going, when it would be convenient to go, and how much it is estimated to cost. I would also hope that you have a certain assurance from the Lord that this is His will for you. Your burden to follow the Lord's leading is what will keep you from quitting when things get tough. There are three parts to biblical support raising.
1.   Do your part. If the trip is important to you, put your money where your mouth is. Be willing to personally sacrifice. Sacrifice includes saving earned money instead of splurging.

2.   Let God do His part. Continue to tithe and give offerings. Do not take your normal giving and apply it to your own self in the name of missions. Be faithful to Christ and let Him do more with your leftovers than you could do with the whole. Pray and seek God's blessing.

3.   Ask others for help. Most people have a hard time with this because asking reveals weakness. But refusing to ask reveals a pride issue. You would be surprised at how many other people will want to help you. Share your story. Tell people about who you are going to visit, where you are going, how you plan to get there, when you would like to go, what you would be doing, and how much more you are trying to raise. As the Lord leads, you can directly ask someone to help you financially, or indirectly mention the needs and let God do the work in his/her heart. For those who are too young to have a job, fund raisers are another great way to work at earning the funds as well as give a benefit to the donors. Do not discount your prayer partners. You will have more people willing to pray for you than give to help you get there. They are as important if not more so than those who give monetarily.

4.   Keep track of all of your funds. Record them in a book for a two-fold reason. First, a record shows you to be a good steward of the finances. And if the trip gets completely cancelled for some reason, it enables you to return the funds to your sponsors. A record keeps you blameless from accusations regarding misused money. Second, this record becomes a prayer and praise journal that you will be able to go back to and relish in the goodness of God. For every gift and prayer partner, thank the Lord. When times get tough, you can turn through the pages and remember how God is able to meet your every need no matter how big or small.

What to Do on the Trip?
1.   As you pray, plan, and prepare, you should also be in correspondence with the missionary that you will visit. Make yourself available to do anything. Remember to be a servant. You will also need to be flexible when (not if) things do not go according to planned. Having a general idea of activities gives you something to share with those who may be sponsoring you. It also gives you more specific details that you can pray over. The two greatest abilities you can possess are availability and flexibility. God can mightily use weak vessels who are yielded to His power.
2.   It is useful to keep a journal of notes during your trip. A time of private writing is an excellent means of reflecting on what God is doing during your trip. A journal also serves as a good reminder after your trip of what all took place. The bodily fatigue and time constraint are not conducive to naturally remembering things simply by memory.

3.　　　When you take your trip, enjoy yourself. Have fun. Takes lots of pictures as opportunity permits but do not forget your primary purpose. Hang onto the memories. Let Jesus work in your heart before, during, and after the trip. Seek for God to teach you along the way. Look for God to show you His plan for your life. Share your adventure with others to keep it fresh.

QUICK TIPS FOR TRIPS

1. Be advised that the trip relayed in this book, tips suggested for travel, and the section on how to plan a mission trip is prior to Covid-19 restrictions and requirements.

2. Your luggage might not make it. Pack every initially essential item in your carry-on. Spread out where you keep your cash in case a bag goes missing.

3. Your very important things need to go in an inner pocket of your luggage. If for example, a thief slices the bottom of your backpack, an inner pocket needs to prevent your most important valuables from falling out.

4. If you utilize a backpack, zip all your zippers to one side so that you need only give great attention to watching one side. If you have a partner with whom you can walk side by side, zip your zippers on the side toward each other so that no pick pocketers can easily get into your possessions.

5. Luggage locks are advisable but expect them to be taken off and lost.

6. Make a photocopy of your passport and put it in each piece of luggage in case of needing to identify lost luggage. Keeping a photocopy of each other's passports or having a designated person do so is advisable in case a passport goes missing and can be replaced easier at a U.S. consulate.

7. If a taxi driver places luggage on the roof, watch the back window and mirrors to ensure nothing falls off. I watched this take place on one of my trips.

8. I do not recommend using a belly band for carrying your passport; it is extremely uncomfortable and inconvenient. Consider carrying your passport in a necklace styled carrier. Keep your wallet, phone, etc. in front pockets, never back pockets.

9. If you do not want to arrive overseas so sleep deprived, consider a lengthy layover and spending the night outside of the airport in a hotel.

10. Prolonged exposure to different kinds of food tends to result in diarrhea as your body gets used to the new food (not necessarily bad food). Some sort of an anti-diarrhea medicine is wise to take with you. Take along other medicine for colds, flu, headache, etc.

11. Plan how you will communicate to family or friends back home that you are safe, secure, or in an emergency. Internet is fairly common, but not completely everywhere.

12. Print your itinerary with details of where you are staying, how long you are staying, and expected modes of transportation. Leave said itinerary in the hands of trusted friends or family, as well as take a copy with you as your own guide.

13. Be advised that most countries use 220 voltage instead of the standard 110 in the U.S. Some products require a converter and other products are being produced to accept either voltage.

14. Never appear lost, unless you are asking someone for directions. Lost folks are prey to thieves. Act like a foreign country is your country and even pretend like you know where you are and what you are doing.

ABOUT THE AUTHORS

R. A. Beaulacotte was born and raised in California. He grew up in a Christian home with the erroneous pre-conceived idea that going to Sunday school and being in a Christian family automatically made him a Christian and on his way to heaven. At the age of approximately seven years old, being the year 2005, he finally came to the knowledge of Jesus Christ through a gospel tract and the explaining of the gospel by his mother.

Because everyone sins, everybody starts out on their way to hell with a debt that cannot be paid by anything they can do. The good news is that God took on Himself the form of flesh. He was known as Jesus Christ while walking upon this earth. The God-man, Jesus, lived a sinless life to earn people a way into heaven. But He also died to pay for every sin, was buried, and rose again according to prophecies which were written down thousands of years prior. R. A. Beaulacotte turned from trusting in his Christian heritage, to trusting in Jesus alone for his salvation.

Now he lives each day with the peace of God and blessed assurance of going to heaven one day, not by anything he accomplished, but solely because of what Jesus has already done on his behalf.

As R. A. Beaulacotte was entering his teenage years, the Lord called him to preach. When he was fifteen years old, his family moved to Maui, Hawaii whereupon a great deal of events have transpired, all leading him closer to the center of God's will.

When he was sixteen years old, he took his first trip out of the country to Nepal which you can read about in *Journey to the Himalayas.* Then, when he was eighteen years old, he took this trip to the Philippines. R. A. Beaulacotte has since graduated from Bible college, finished linguistic training, got married, has a child, and is currently going back to Asia to be a missionary. Serving the King of Kings is not only the greatest duty of man, but also the highest privilege and blessing. To God be the glory, both now and always.

R. A. Beaulacotte Sr. grew up in catholic churches and schools in Montana. In his college years in California, he was searching for meaning and feeling alone. It came about that one day as he was leaving campus, a person was passing out small New Testament Bibles. He took that little Bible home and started reading it. He was like a dry sponge soaking up living water. His heart and mind were eager for the truth of God. Already frustrated by the failures to find fulfilment in education and money, he put his faith in Jesus. One night in September 1979 age 22, God showed him he needed what Jesus did on the cross for his sins. So, he called out to Jesus to save him and thanked Jesus for his work on the cross for his sins.

Now, by the grace of God, R.A. Beaulacotte Sr. lives for Christ. He is committed to the conviction that we are in the last days approaching the return of Christ. He strongly believes that Christians need to redeem their time, abilities, and resources for Jesus Christ and His Kingdom.

Made in the USA
Monee, IL
29 August 2021